A

PICTURE
STORY BOOK
FOR
GROWNUPS

WITH

MUSIC

DEDICATED TO

FAMILIES

AND TO

FATHER GOD

WHO, AFTER ALL, STARTED IT!!

They Did what?

ISBN 978-0-9701493-5-0

Printed in the United States of America

Contents

HOW IT ALL BEGAN

"A BLIND DATE??"
"BUT MOM..."

"HE'S IN THE AIR FORCE AND A LONG WAY FROM HOME! HE'S
FROM WEST VIRGINIA AND PROBABLY HOMESICK, MOM!!"

"MOM AND DAD SAID I COULD GO, WENDELL, BUT I HAVE TO BE
HOME BY 10:30 p.m."

THAT FIRST DATE INCLUDED A MOVIE AND A SANDWICH LATER. THE
RESTAURANT WHERE WE ATE HAD A JUKE BOX AND WENDELL
PLAYED A TUNE THAT I LOVED ....

"HEY, GOOD LOOKIN'
WHAT CHA GOT A COOKIN'...

THAT WAS THE START THEN OF FOOTBALL GAMES, SCHOOL DANCES,
PICNICS, FAMILY DRIVES INTO THE MOUNTAINS AND IN JUNE, AT
THE SENIOR PROM WHILE THE BAND WAS PLAYING ....

"STARDUST"

WENDELL OWLAND ALEXANDER ASKED
ME TO MARRY HIM, EVEN THOUGH IT CAME OUT ....

"WELL, DARN IT MARY,
I LOVE YA!!"

AN ENGAGEMENT RING FOLLOWED. ALSO, 18 MONTHS IN
FARAWAY JAPAN WHERE WENDELL WAS TRANSFERRED TO AN AIR BASE!

井上貴金属店

THE BIG DAY ARRIVED

THE LONG AWAITED EVENT MADE THE SUNDAY NEWSPAPER ALSO!

The Bride Gets a Wheelbarrow Ride

Photo for The Denver Post by Larche

Mrs. Mary Lou Alexander clings to a jolting wheelbarrow pushed by her husband of only a few minutes, Wendell Alexander, as they fall victim to prankish relatives after their wedding Saturday at St. Vincent de Paul Catholic Church. The wheelbarrow ride followed the Alexanders' discovery that the pranksters had jacked up the rear of their car and propped it high in the air with stacks of bricks. The bride is formerly Mary Lou TeMaat.

"COUNTRY ROADS TAKE ME HOME ..."

WE DID GO TO WENDELL'S HOME IN WEST VIRGINIA FOR OUR HONEYMOON;
WELL, AFTER WE GOT THE CAR DOWN OFF THE BRICKS THAT IS!!

WE SETTLED DOWN IN DENVER THEN WITH OUR BUNDLES OF JOY ARRIVING
ONE AFTER THE OTHER • • • • UNTIL • • •

EIGHT BUNDLES OF JOY LATER

..."HAPPY ANNIVERSARY DAD AND MOM, HAPPY ELEVENTH ANNIVERSARY TO YOU."

ONE OF OUR THEME SONGS THEN WAS,

"OH, WE AIN'T GOT A BARREL OF MONEY...

"WHEN WHIPPOORWILLS

CALL AND EVENING IS NIGH,

I HURRY TO
        MY BLUE HEAVEN....."

JUST WENDELL AND ME, AND

BABIES MAKES TEN

WE'RE HAPPY IN

        OUR BLUE HEAVEN"

"THEY DID WHAT??"

"PAINTED EACH OTHER WITH BROWN
ENAMEL PAINT?"

"HA, HA, HA!!"

HOW CAN THE DOCTOR LAUGH LIKE THAT?

THIS IS A SERIOUS SITUATION. THESE

THREE KIDS OF MINE HAVE PAINTED EACH

OTHER WITH ....

BROWN

ENAMEL

PAINT!!

THE PAINT IS DRYING!

THE KIDS ARE STANDING

IN THE BATHTUB

CRYING! NO!!

THEY ARE ....

YELLING!!

"MAMA, MAMA, MY SKIN IS ITCHING."

"MAMA, GET IT OFF!!" "IT HURTS."

THE DOCTOR, HEARING THE KIDS IN THE BACKGROUND AND
TRYING TO REASSURE ME, SAYS, "MRS. ALEXANDER, IT WILL BE
OKAY." "COCONUT OIL WILL GET IT OFF."

I HEAR A MUFFLED LAUGH COMING FROM THE OTHER END OF THE
PHONE. "THANKS, DOCTOR," I SAY, "I'LL TRY THAT."

AFTER A CALL TO THE NEXT DOOR NEIGHBOR TO WATCH THE
KIDS; AN EXPENSIVE TRIP TO THE CORNER DRUG
STORE FOR A BOTTLE OF COCONUT OIL AND ....

IT DID'NT WORK!!

ANOTHER CALL TO ANOTHER NEIGHBOR WHOSE HUSBAND
WAS A PROFESSIONAL HOUSE PAINTER;

AN HOUR AND A

HALF SCRUBBING

WITH LANOLIN

PAINT REMOVER!!

THREE VERY PINK AND VERY APOLOGETIC LITTLE PEOPLE
CAME OUT OF THE BATHROOM SAYING,
"MAMA, WE WON'T EVER GET INTO DADDY'S
PAINT AGAIN, "

"NEVER

AGAIN,

MAMA!!"

"ALL TEN OF US??"
"ON THE TRAIN??"
"TO CHICAGO??"

IT HAPPENED!! AT 5:37 P.M. ON A FRIDAY AFTERNOON, ALL TEN OF US LEFT THE DENVER TRAIN DEPOT HEADING FOR GRANDPA AND GRANDMA'S HOUSE IN CHICAGO, ILLINOIS.

ALL WENT WELL FOR ABOUT ....

22 MINUTES!!

THE OLDER KIDS STARTED THE INVESTIGATION FIRST; FINDING THEIR SEATS' MECHANISM THAT WENT ....

DOWN!!   UP!!   LAY DOWN!!

"I NEED A DRINK OF WATER, DAD!!"

"OK", SAYS WENDELL TO OUR YOUNGEST DAUGHTER, MADELEINE. THEN REBECCA, OUR SECOND TO THE YOUNGEST SAYS, "ME TOO, DAD". "OK", HE SAYS AGAIN.

LITTLE DID WE KNOW THE ATTRACTION OF THE WATER FOUNTAIN'S HIGH POWERED SPIGOT!

WE SHOULD HAVE KNOWN THE CAR IN FRONT OF OURS WOULD BE A GREAT ATTRACTION. AS WENDELL AND I LOOKED UP FROM THE WATER FOUNTAIN SCENE, COMING FROM THE

DINER, LOADED DOWN WITH POP AND CANDY

WERE THERESA, DE ANN AND TIM!!

"DAD!"

"HEY, DAD!!"

RAYMOND IS CALLING.
"I NEED

MY COMIC BOOKS, OKAY?"
AND BEFORE WENDELL COULD SAY
OR DO ANYTHING, UP ON THE
SHOULDERS OF CHRIS, RAY
HOPS, OPENING THE OVERHEAD
BAGGAGE COMPARTMENT AND INTO
ONE OF THE SUITCASES
SEARCHING FOR THE COMICS,
CLOTHES FLYING EVERYWHERE.

"TICKETS, HAVE YOUR TICKETS READY!!"

ABOUT THAT TIME, THE TRAIN'S
CONDUCTOR IS COLLECTING
TICKETS IN OUR CAR. HE IS
LOOKING AT ALL THE CHILDRENS'
ACTIVITY, THEN LOOKING AT

PASSENGER'S COUPON	NON-TRANSFERABLE Sold Subject to Tariff Regulations

NOT GOOD FOR PASSAGE
OF CLASS SHOWN
VIA RAILROAD INDICATED BY ☒

From **DENVER, COLO.**

To.. ch.i.cAgo, I.ll....

ONE WAY	ROUND TRIP	FIRST CLASS	COACH CLASS	GOVERN- MENT
☐	☒	☐	☐	☐

FAMILY TICKET

AT & SF	D & R G W	
CB & Q	UN. PAC.	

GOOD FOR	ADULTS	CHILDREN 12 to 21 incl.	CHILDREN 5 to 11-incl.	TOTAL
	2	3	4	9

ENDORSEMENTS
1 child 4 yrs.
free

FORM 10	64552	DATE EXPIRES 6 mo 19 69

SELLING AGENT
STAMP HERE
65.45
43.65
43.65
43.65
43.65   327.85
21.95
21.95   Total $
21.95
21.95
327.85   BAGGAGE ☐

Issued by THE DENVER UNION TERMINAL RY. CO.

L. E. Merz   Ticket Agent DENVER, COLO.   **DUT**

OUR TICKET, SAYS TO MY HUSBAND,

"ALL THESE KIDS YOURS??"
"MUST HAVE COST YOU
A FORTUNE, MAC!!"

"YOU BETTER BELIEVE IT, MISTER,"   WENDELL SAYS.

BEFORE THE TRIP ENDED, THE KIDS KNEW THE CONDUCTOR BY NAME, THE
COOKS NAME IN THE DINING CAR, THE ENGINEER'S AND THE
PORTER'S NAME.

NOT MUCH SLEEP THAT NIGHT IN OUR CAR. THE OLDER KIDS HAD
ENGAGED HALF THE PEOPLE IN SONG AND STORY-TELLING.

"SHE'LL BE COM'IN 'ROUND
THE MOUNTAIN WHEN SHE
COMES..."

SEVENTEEN HOURS AND 10 MINUTES LATER, WE ARE GREETED AT THE
CHICAGO TRAIN STATION BY WENDELL'S FAMILY.
TEN DAYS LATER, WE ARE GREETED BY MY FAMILY IN THE DENVER
DEPOT. "HOW WAS THE TRIP EVERYBODY?" MY MOM SAYS.
ALL THE KIDS ARE TALKING AT ONCE TELLING ABOUT THE TRAIN
RIDE AND ALL THE FUN THEY HAD IN CHICAGO.

WENDELL AND I ARE LOOKING AT EACH OTHER, SMILING. "YEAH,
IT WAS FUN!!" "REALLY!" "REALLY??"
"REALLY!!"

Chicago Train Ride . . . 1969

THERESA

CHRIS

DE ANN

MONICA

TIM

MADELEINE

WENDELL

REBECCA

MARY LOU

RAY

Back home . . .

A new recipe for dinner . . .
and disaster!

EGGPLANT, MOM?
YUK!

10:30 A.M.

YOU KIDS ARE GOING TO LOVE IT! I FOUND A GREAT RECIPE IN
THE NEWSPAPER AND IT REALLY SOUNDS LIKE IT WILL BE GOOD.

5:30 P.M.

SUPPERTIME - MENU: HAMBURGER PATTIES, EGGPLANT PARMESAN AND
ICE CREAM.

5:32 P.M.

EVERYONE HAS DISHED UP FOOD ON PLATES. BLESSING IS SAID.

5:34 P.M.

TIM UP-CHUCKS EGG PLANT PARMESAN BACK INTO HIS PLATE.

5:34½ P.M.

WENDELL LEAVES THE TABLE, HEADING FOR THE BATHROOM. SO MUCH
FOR THE NEW RECIPE I TELL MYSELF. "HOW ABOUT
THE ICE CREAM KIDS?"

BYE DAD.

WENDELL, YOU OK?

URRPP

Loved those pets

that lived with us!

AS I PULLED A LOAD
OF CLOTHES OUT
OF THE CLOTHES DRYER,

"I FOUND THE SNAKE!"

"AGAIN, THE SCREEN DOOR IS BROKEN AGAIN??"

WENDELL IS STANDING ON THE BACK PORCH LOOKING AT THE BROKEN
SCREEN DOOR HE HAD JUST FIXED AN HOUR BEFORE.

OUR CAT "FLUFFLY" HAD COME INTO THE HOUSE
WITH A BIRD IN HIS MOUTH. MORGAN,
OUR DOG, SPIED THE CAT'S TREASURE AND
PROCEEDED TO RUN AFTER BOTH. THE CAT
DROPS THE BIRD; THE BIRD TAKES
FLIGHT AROUND THE HOUSE FROM ONE
ROOM TO THE OTHER; THE CAT CHASING
THE BIRD, THE DOG CHASING
THE CAT AND THE KIDS CHASING
ALL THREE.

FINALLY, THE BIRD LANDS ON THE SCREEN
WITH THE CAT JUMPING UP ON IT TO
GET THE BIRD AND THE DOG MAKING THE
FINAL LEAP; ALL THREE GO THROUGH THE
SCREEN DOOR. SIX OF THE KIDS
RUNNING THROUGH THE SAME SPOT.

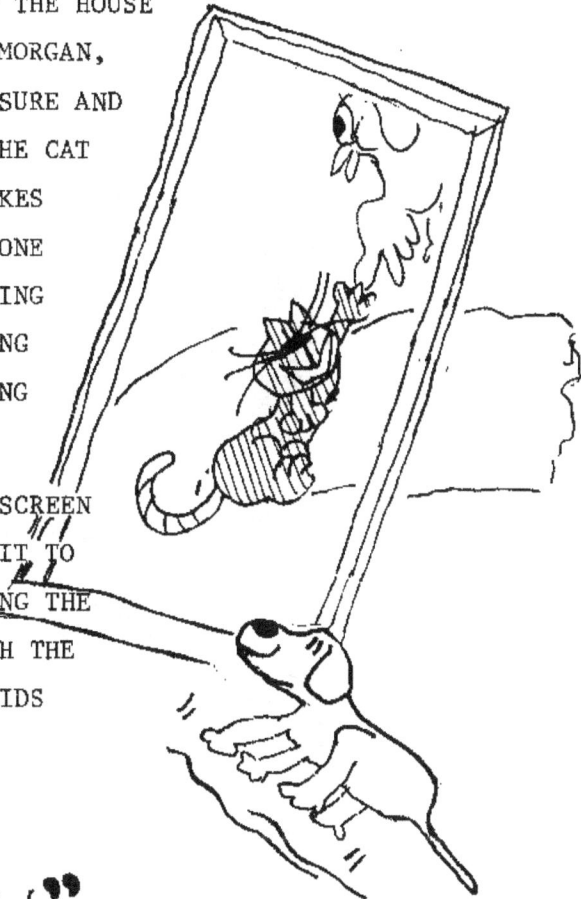

"GOOD BYE SCREEN DOOR!!"

Oh . . . and then there were all those wonderful HOLIDays . . .

HEY-LOOK MOM! IT'S MARY, JOSEPH, BABY JESUS AND THOSE 3 WISE GUYS!

when shopping was even more fun than usual . . .

"HONEY, WE'RE OUT OF TOOTHPASTE", CALLS MY HUSBAND FROM THE BATHROOM. "MOM," "MOM", "HEY, MOM", HOLLERS ONE OF THE GIRLS FROM THE BASEMENT BATHROOM, "WE'RE DOWN TO ONE SHAMPOO".

SEEMS LIKE WE WE'RE ALWAYS OUT OF TOOTHPASTE OR SHAMPOO ALL THE TIME. WELL, WE RAN OUT OF OTHER STUFF TOO, SUCH AS:

TOILET PAPER BANANAS BREAD PEANUTBUTTER
MILK SHAMPOO
DOG FOOD POPCORN JELLY
CEREAL COOKIES

I'M GOING SHOPPING.

MOM, I WANT A NEW SLED.

GET ME A TRAIN SET MOM.

I WANNA NINTENDO GAME MOM.

HEY! I'M JUST BUYING GROCERIES.

"ONE OF THE FAVORITE TIMES OF THE YEAR, BESIDES CHRISTMAS THAT IS!!"

"LOVE WINTER MONTHS!!"

and then of course
there was summer . . .

"WATER FIGHT!!"

"WATER FIGHT!!"

I CAN HEAR THE HOLLERING FROM THE BACK YARD!! WHAT HAD
STARTED OUT TO BE A "QUIET" YARD CLEANING SATURDAY MORNING
WAS TURNING INTO A SQUIRTING MATCH WITH THE FRONT AND BACK
YARD HOSES. LAWN MOWING, RAKING AND GENERAL CLEAN UP OF THE
YARD WAS ABOUT DONE WHEN WENDELL CAME AROUND THE CORNER OF
THE HOUSE WITH THE FRONT YARD HOSE AND STARTED SQUIRTING THE
KIDS IN THE BACK YARD. ONE OF THE KIDS GRABBED THE BACK
YARD HOSE, ANOTHER ONE TURNED IT
ON, BUT BY THE TIME THEY GOT THE
WATER GOING THEIR DAD WAS OUT OF
REACH. "CHICKEN!!"
"YOUR A
CHICKEN, DAD!"

"WE'LL GET YOU DAD, JUST WAIT

AND

SEE!!"

OH, DID THEY GET THEIR DAD!! HA, HA!

ONE OF THE BOYS CLIMBED UP ON THE ROOF OF THE BACKPORCH WITH A PAN FULL OF WATER; THE OTHER KIDS WERE IN THE YARD PLAYING....

THEY KNEW THEIR DAD HAD TO COME OUT OF THE HOUSE SOONER OR LATER. OUT HE CAME!

DOWN CAME THE WATER AND DID HE GET A SOAKING. WE ALL SPLIT OUR SIDES LAUGHING.

HE SAID,

"OK YOU KIDS, WE'RE EVEN!!"

and the "business" of life!

"JOBS?? YOU'RE KIDDING, DAD!!"

"THATS RIGHT, KIDS. NOW THAT MOM IS WORKING YOU WILL HAVE TO HELP OUT WITH THE CHORES."

DAILY JOBS								
	CHRIS	TIM	DE ANN	MONICA	RAY	THERESA	REBECCA	MADELEINE
MON	1	2	3	4	5	6	1	2
TUES	2	3	4	5	6	1	2	3
WED	3	4	5	6	1	2	3	4
THURS	4	5	6	1	2	3	4	5
FRI	5	6	1	2	3	4	5	6
SAT	6	1	2	3	4	5	6	1
SUN	7	7	7	7	7	7	7	7

1. Dishes
2. Trash
3. Dog Doodie
4. Bathrooms
5. Livingroom
6. Diningroom
7. Church

IF YOU'LL TRADE JOBS WITH ME, I'LL GIVE YOU TWO CANDY BARS

"FIXING LUNCHES FOR SCHOOL WAS ALWAYS FUN!!??"

then . . .

first Mom

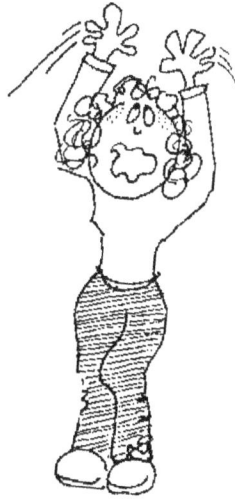

and next Dad

took little "vacations"

"MOMS HOME !!"

"HI MOM!" "HI MA !!"

"GLAD YOUR HOME, MOM!"

"SURE GOOD TO BE HOME TOO, EVERYBODY.""SEEMS LIKE I WAS GONE FOR
SIX MONTHS NOT JUST SIX WEEKS; AND THAT WAS NOT MY IDEA OF
A VACATION BEING IN THE HOSPITAL." "WHAT WAS THE MATTER WITH
YOUR NERVE, MOM?" "DAD SAID YOUR NERVE WAS SICK". "THATS RIGHT,
YOU KIDS, MY NERVE WAS JUMBLED UP AND I NEEDED A REST.THE
DOCTOR SAID."

OUR OLDEST SON SAID, "MOM, I THOUGHT SOMETHING WAS UP WHEN
YOU PUT THE IRON IN THE REFRIGERATOR AND THE GALLON BOTTLE OF
MILK IN THE LINEN CLOSET". "THAT WAS STRANGE WASN'T IT?",
I SAID. I FEEL BETTER NOW, BUT I AM GOING TO HAVE TO TAKE
IT EASY FOR AWHILE.

"WHAT HELPERS I HAD!"

"HOW SPECIAL. . . . . BREAKFAST
IN BED. CAKE, POPCORN . . OH NO,
COLD PIZZA TOO!"

"THE DOCTOR SAID I HAD AN ALCOHOL ALLERGY, KIDS, AND I NEEDED TO STAY IN THE HOSPITAL THAT LONG." . "SURE GOOD TO BE HOME."

YOU ARE CORDIALLY INVITED

TO ATTEND

THE ANNUAL SUPPORT GROUP

DINNER

••WENDELL ALEXANDER••
MASTER OF
CEREMONIES

• MARY LOU ALEXANDER •
SING . A . LONG
GAMES

•••ALEXANDER CHILDREN•••
SINGING

THEIR FAVORITE SONGS

FAMOUS TRUMPET PLAYER
OUT CHICAGO WAY.... HE'S
THE BOOGIE WOOGIE BUGLE BOY..

OF   MADS   TECEE   BECCA

COMPANY

"THE HOUSE WAS GETTING TOO SMALL, TIME FOR A CHANGE!!"

THE REALTOR IS COMING OVER WITH A PROSPECTIVE BUYER, WHEN?!

"THE TRUCKS HERE!!"

"THE TRUCKS HERE!!"

THE BIG DAY FINALLY ARRIVED! NEW FURNITURE FOR THE LIVING
ROOM. AFTER THE DELIVERY MEN LEFT ALL TEN OF US TOOK
TURNS SITTING ON THE COUCH AND CHAIR: TURNING THE NEW
LAMP ON AND OFF AND THE GIRLS PUTTING KNICK KNACKS ON THE
NEW SIDE TABLE AND THE COFFEE TABLE.

EARLIER IN THE DAY MY HUSBAND HAD MADE A

NEW FRIEND!

A HUGE GREY AND BLACK DOG. WE ALL AGREED HE WAS FRIENDLY
ENOUGH, WAGGING HIS TAIL AND LICKING THE KIDS'FACES. THE DOG
WAS IN THE HOUSE WHEN THE NEW FURNITURE ARRIVED.

"SUPPERTIME!!"

ABOUT AN HOUR LATER, I CALLED EVERYONE TO SIT DOWN AND EAT.
WENDELL WAS TELLING THE KIDS THE DOG PROBABLY BELONGED
TO A FAMILY IN THE NEIGHBORHOOD AND AFTER WE ATE, WE WOULD
HAVE TO PUT THE DOG OUTSIDE. BEING THE FIRST ONE UP FROM
THE TABLE, HE WENT INTO THE LIVINGROOM. HALF A MINUTE
LATER HE LET OUT A BLOOD CURDLING YELL....

OUT!

OUT! YOU MUTT!

WE ALL RAN INTO THE LIVINGROOM AND SAW WHAT WENDELL WAS YELLING
ABOUT. THE "NEW FOUND FRIEND" HAD CHEWED A BIG HOLE RIGHT
IN THE ARM OF THE NEW COUCH. EVERYONE AGREED, NO MORE STRAY
ANIMALS!!!!

our priest blessed
the new house . . .

and the games began anew!

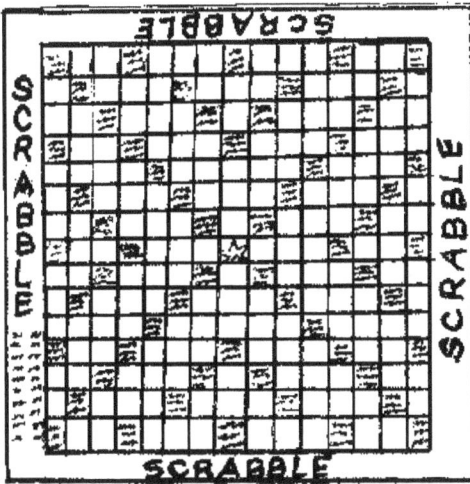

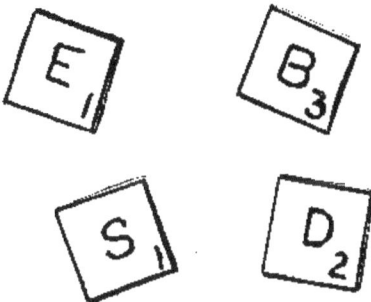

THE SUPER BOWL
OF SCRABBLE
WAS KICKED OFF

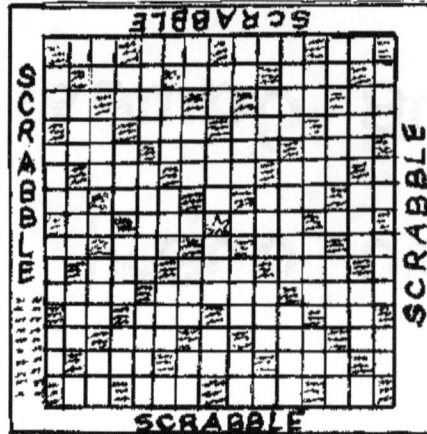

WHEN ONE OF THE KIDS USED ALL
SEVEN OF THEIR TILES TO SPELL
A WORD, MOANS AND GROANS COULD
BE HEARD ALL AROUND THE ROOM.
THE FIRST ANNUAL ALEXANDER
SCRABBLE TOURNAMENT HAD BEGUN IN ERNEST WITH THREE SCRABBLE
BOARDS, FOUR ALEXANDERS AT EACH BOARD, PLUS TWO OF THE KIDS'
FRIENDS JOINING US.

EVERYONE WAS LOOKING FORWARD TO BREAKING   RECORDS IN SOME
OF THE CATEGORIES WE HAD SET UP OVER THE YEARS.

I'LL TELL YOU WHAT THEY ARE:

"MOST GAME POINTS WHEN 4 PEOPLE ARE PLAYING"

"LONGEST WORD"

"MOST GAMES WON IN A ROW"

"HIGHEST SCORED WORD"

"HIGHEST SCORE FOR ONE LETTER PLAYED"

"HIGHEST SCORE FOR TWO WORDS MADE AT ONE TIME"

"HIGHEST SCORE FOR THREE WORDS MADE AT ONE TIME"

"HIGHEST SCORE FOR A 30 MINUTE GAME (WENDELL WAS
          TIRED THAT NIGHT AND GAME ONLY LASTED 30
          MINUTES)

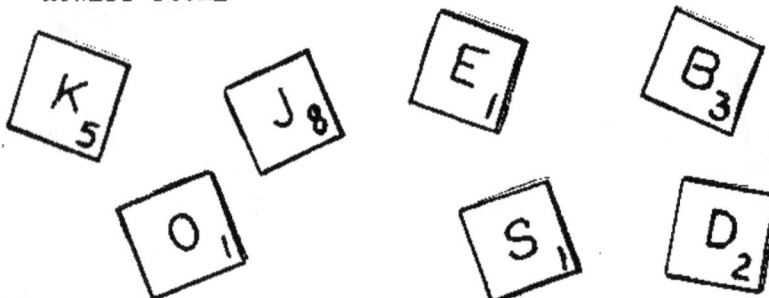

"LOWEST SCORE"

"REMEMBER THE RULE, DAD, ONLY ONE FREE LOOK IN THE DICTIONARY!!"

"WATCH THE HOURGLASS TOO, DAD, ONLY THREE MINUTES A TURN!!"

BY THE END OF THE DAY, THE TOURNAMENT ENDED
WITH THREE HIGH-SCORE PLAYERS WINNING
THE GRAND PRIZES;

THREE OFFICIAL "SCRABBLE" DICTIONARIES!!

"AND, YES, SOME RECORDS WERE BROKEN!!"

HAIR CUTS?
COME ON MOM,
ITS THE STYLE!

DURING ONE PARTICULAR LOOOOOONNNNGGG
SUMMER, THE BOYS DECIDED TO ADD ZEST
TO THEIR LIVES BY LETTING THEIR HAIR

G

   R

      O

        W.

AFTER TWO MONTHS, I
FINALLY SAID AT THE BREAKFAST
TABLE ONE MORNING, "OKAY
BOYS, I GIVE YOU EXACTLY THREE WEEKS TO GET THAT HAIR CUT. IF THAT
HAIR IS NOT CUT BY THAT TIME I AM GOING TO SNEAK DOWN IN YOUR
BEDROOM WHEN YOU'RE ASLEEP AND CUT IT OFF MYSELF."

THREE WEEKS IS UP!
11:00 O'CLOCK A.M.

THE BOYS WERE AT THE BALL FIELD, I WENT DOWNSTAIRS AND UNLOCKED
THE WINDOW TO THEIR BEDROOM, DECIDING THEY HAD NOT TAKEN
MY WARNING SERIOUSLY,   I WAS GETTING PREPARED!

11:45 O'CLOCK P.M.

QUIETLY I RAISED THE WINDOW AND CLIMBED INTO THEIR ROOM. REACHING
UP TO THE TOP BUNK, I TOOK A HANDFUL OF HAIR THAT WAS LAYING ON

THE PILLOW, "OH, OH," I SAID TO MYSELF, THE BOYS HAD A FRIEND
SPEND THE NIGHT AND IT WAS HIS HAIR I HAD A HOLD OF. BY NOW, I'M
TRYING NOT TO LAUGH TOO LOUD, BUT TO NO AVAIL.

"MOMS IN THE   HA

HA

HA   ROOM, MOMS IN

HA

HA   THE ROOM"   HA

THE LIGHT SWITCH WENT ON. TWO CHAIRS HAD BEEN SHOVED UP AGAINST
THE DOOR AND THAT MADE ME LAUGH EVEN MORE. "HOW DID YOU
GET IN HERE MOM," THEY WERE ALL SAYING AT ONE TIME. "YOU'LL
NEVER KNOW!" HA, HA. I TOLD THE KID WHO SPENT THE NIGHT, "YOU
ALMOST GOT A FREE HAIRCUT, FRIEND."

WE WERE ALL LAUGHING BY THEN AND AFTER THAT NIGHT I DECIDED THE
LONG HAIR WASN'T THAT IMPORTANT ANYHOW!

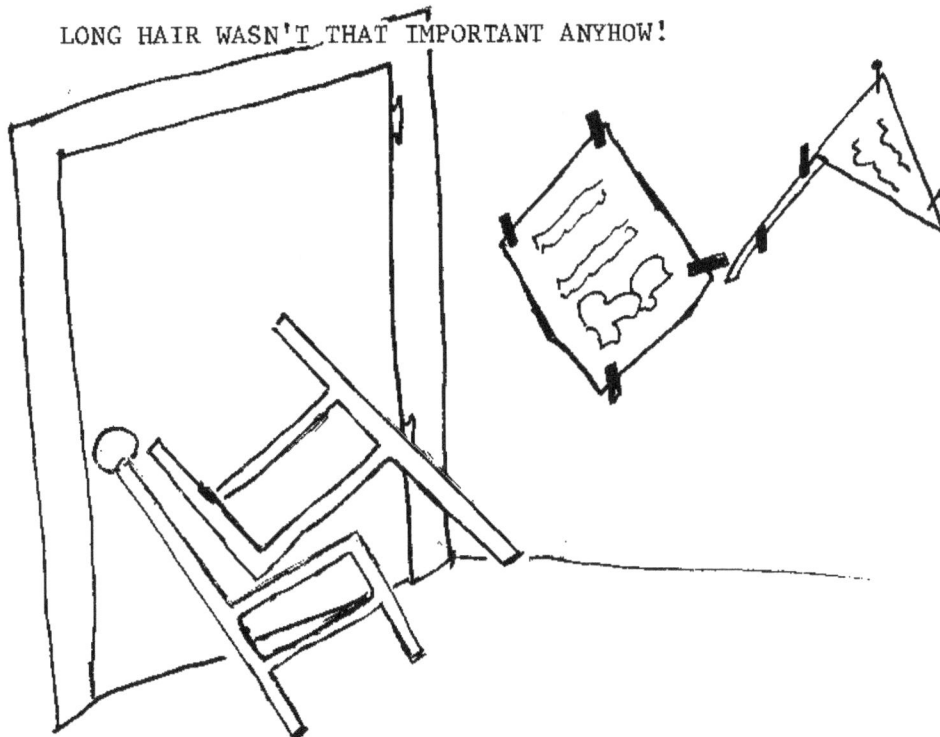

"A NEW HIP MOM??"

"WOW, NEAT!!"

I HAD JUST GOTTEN HOME FROM THE DOCTOR'S OFFICE AND WAS TELLING
THE KIDS AND MY HUSBAND THAT THE DOCTOR WAS GOING TO PUT
A NEW HIP IN ME, BECAUSE THE OLD ONE WAS WORN OUT!!

I COULD NOT FEEL THE CHILDREN'S ENTHUSIASM THOUGH, BECAUSE I
WAS **"SCARED"**

ONE OF THE KIDS COULD SEE
MY "SCARED" AND SAID, "BUT, MOM,
REMEMBER WHEN I WAS DOING
THE SCARY FENCE CLIMBING AND I
REMINDED YOU WHAT YOU TOLD ME
ABOUT OUR GUARDIAN ANGELS,"

"YOUR ANGEL

WILL

TAKE

CARE OF

YOU TOO,

MOM!!"

"LESSONS ON PRAYER..."

"HAROLD, BE THY NAME..."

YOU MEAN "HOLLOWED BE THY NAME," HONEY, I SAY TO MY SON TRYING
NOT TO LAUGH. "BUT, MAYBE GOD'S NAME IS HAROLD, MOM!",
HE SAYS. "I NEVER THOUGHT ABOUT GOD HAVING A NAME, COULD BE."

AS WE CONTINUE THE ROSARY I BEGIN TO LISTEN MORE INTENTLY TO
WHAT THE CHILDREN ARE SAYING........

"THE FOURTH GLORIOUS
MYSTERY,
MARY IS ZOOMED INTO HEAVEN!!"

"HAIL HOLY QUEEN,
MOTHER OF MURPHY,"

"ST. MICHAEL,
THE PARK RANGER...."

"LEARNING LESSONS ABOUT THE BIBLE..."

"MORE BIBLE LESSONS.."

and at the church . . .

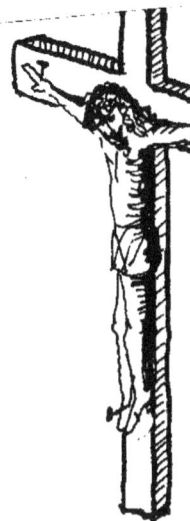

"LESSONS IN BATHROOM ETIQUETTE"

"LEARNED

THROUGH

TRIAL

AND

ERROR"

"MORE ABOUT THE BATHROOM.."

WHERE DID I PUT THAT COMB!

"ALRIGHT, DAD, WE'RE READY TO SHAVE NOW"

"THEY SAID WHAT...??"

ASK ME NO QUESTIONS AND I'LL TELL YOU NO LIES.

"BUT DOCTOR, MY "FROAT" IS SORE..."

"AND..."

"AND THEN THEY SAID..."

MOM, CAN I PET THE NEW BABY?

"MAMA, AM I GONNA GET MY SHOCKS TOO?"

"AND ALSO...."

Then Mom and Dad
took a long overdue
vacation together . . .

SECOND HONEYMOON,

HERE WE COME!!

ONE BY ONE THE CHILDREN LEFT THE NEST.
MY HUSBAND AND I DECIDED OUR HOUSE
HAD GOTTEN TOO BIG; THE MOUNTAINS
CALLING US TOO OFTEN; SO AFTER
MUCH DELIBERATION, WE
MOVED TO A SMALL
MOUNTAIN TOWN
(POPULATION 632). WE
WERE WITHIN TWENTY
MILES WHERE TWO
OF OUR DAUGHTERS,
THEIR HUSBANDS AND THEIR
CHILDREN LIVED, SO WE FELT
WE WEREN'T "RUNNING AWAY FROM
HOME" TOTALLY, AS THE FIVE KIDS
LIVING IN OUR "HOME TOWN"
SUGGESTED. THEY EVEN HAD A BET
WITH OUR TWO MOUNTAINEER
FAMILIES THAT WE WOULD NEVER LAST
THROUGH THE WINTER!

WE FOOLED
THEM!!

wendell was

a GREAT cook!

"WOOPPiiEEE WHAT FUN!!"

NOT ONLY DID WE MAKE IT THROUGH THE WINTER, BUT I TOOK UP CROSS-COUNTRY SKIING AND WENDELL, DOING MOST OF THE COOKING BY NOW IS PLANNING ON OPENING UP HIS OWN RESTAURANT IN THIS MOUNTAIN COMMUNITY. I TOLD HIM, "HE MISSES ALL THOSE KIDS AT THE SUPPER TABLE AND THAT'S WHAT PROMPTED HIM TO START THIS VENTURE!"

→ TURN PAGE

"TRY SOME OF WENDELL OWLAND'S FAVORITE RECIPES!!"

"BREAKFASTS"

EGG-IN-A-HOLE

Cut small hole in bread with "donut
   cutter"
Toast the bread, hole too
Put toasted bread in
   greased pan
Crack open egg and
   place in hole
Turn over once
The hole gets put in
   greased pan too!

BEAN CAKES

Take left-over pinto
   beans from frig,
   put in mixing bowl
Add handful flour
Two eggs
Oil (little bit)
Stir in milk 'til looks like
   pancake mix
Drop by spoonfuls and fry like pancake!

BRAINS & SCRAMBLED EGGS

Fry brains 'til done
Stir eggs in them

Serve especially when kids' friend, Joe Nobles, is here for
   breakfast. "Great breakfast, Mr. Alexander, what was in
     the eggs?" "Cow brains,"says Wendell. Joe runs from
the table, hand over his mouth, out the back door. We didn't
see Joe at the breakfast table for awhile!

FRIED OYSTERS
(Thanksgiving and Christmas Breakfasts)

Dip oysters in flour and place in hot grease
Fry 'til crisp
Make gravy with drippings from oysters
Serve with scrambled eggs and hot biscuits!

"ONE MORE BREAKFAST"

BISCUITS & SAUSAGE GRAVY

Brown crumpled up sausage in fry pan
Add fistful flour to sausage and
   drippings, stir 'til flour is brown
Add water, stir
Salt
Pepper (LOTS OF IT)
Open can biscuits, put in pan, pop
   in oven and bake
Cook gravy 'til done
Serve with eggs (if any left over
   from yesterdays breakfast!

"LUNCHES"

POT-OF-BEANS

Cook two lbs. pinto beans
Add piece of "fat back" and onions
Salt
Pepper (LOTS OF IT)
Cook all day long (about 8 hours)
Serve with fried potatoes
Corn bread
Also, serve anytime with anything!

BEAN/HAMBURGER TORTILLAS

Put left-over pinto beans (again?) in
   fry pan and heat up
Crumble up hamburger and fry with
   chopped onions
Drain juice off beans and add the
   hamburger and onion mixture
Salt
Pepper (LOTS OF IT)
Heat up tortillas
Spread beans, hamburger, onions on warmed up tortillas
Sprinkle with cheese (any kind ya got)
Chopped lettuce next
Add hot sauce (hotter the better)

"SUPPERTIME"

SPAGHETTI 'N MEATBALLS

Lots of tomatoes in pot
Add tomatoe paste
Little garlic
Onions
Any kind spice in cupboard
Cook 'til done (maybe 3 hours)
Fry Italian sausage and put in sauce (crumpled up)
Boil spaghetti - throw against wall, if sticks, it's done
Serve with lettuce, tomatoes, onions, cucumbers and Italian
   dressing
Garlic bread tastes good with this!

ALEXANDER STEW

Brown chunks of beef with onions
Add tomatoes and,
Clean out leftovers in frig
Cook 'til done
Serve hot with biscuits

WENDELL'S FAVORITE MEAL

Meat (any kind)
Potatoes
Gravy
Vegetable
Salad
Bread at every meal
Desert (you can keep it!)

in conclusion then . . .

"LESSONS IN LIVING LIFE!!"

"SAD?"

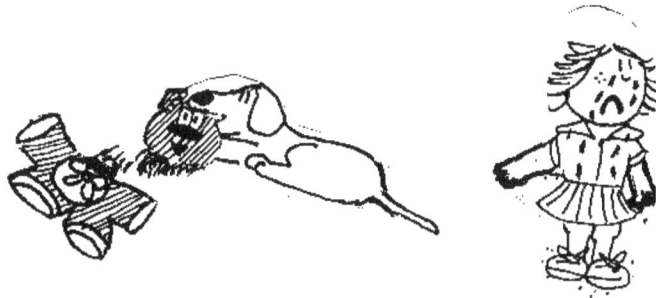

"THINK HAPPY THOUGHTS!"

PHILLIPIANS 4:8

"WHATSOEVER THINGS ARE
TRUE, HONEST, JUST,
PURE, LOVELY; OF GOOD REPORT,
IS VIRTUOUS, AND WORTHY OF
PRAISE, THINK ON THESE THINGS."
(KJV)

"EXCUSE INSTEAD OF ACCUSE!!"

I DID IT MOM! I'M SORRY!

OR

MATTHEW 6:14

YOUR KIDS

"FOR IF YE FORGIVE MEN THEIR
TRESPASSES,
YOUR HEAVENLY FATHER WILL
ALSO FORGIVE YOU."
(KJV Revised by MLA)

"DO THE THING YOU FEAR TO DO!!"

"MAMA, AM I GONNA GET MY SHOCKS TOO?"

I WAS AFRAID OF THAT!

ISAIAH 41:10

"FEAR THOU NOT FOR I AM WITH THEE, BE NOT DISMAYED FOR I AM THY GOD, I WILL HELP THEE YEA, I WILL STRENGTHEN THEE, YEA, I WILL UPHOLD THEE WITH THE RIGHT HAND OF MY RIGHTEOUSNESS." (KJV)

"WORRIED +
ANXIOUS =
TIRED\POOPED"

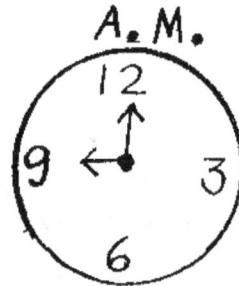

"GET MOVING!!"

"AND KEEP MOVING!!"

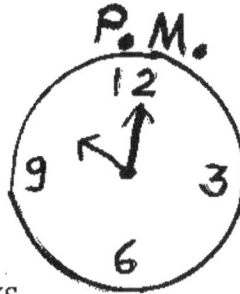

P.M.

JAMES 2:20

"FAITH WITHOUT WORKS
IS DEAD" (KJV)

"IT WAS
HARD
MOVING,
GOD, BUT
I DO FEEL
BETTER
TONIGHT".

sometimes it was
extra easy to . . .

**MORE LESSONS IN LEARNING LIFE!!"

"SOUGHT THROUGH PRAYER AND MEDITATION TO IMPROVE OUR
CONSCIOUS CONTACT WITH GOD AS WE UNDERSTOOD
HIM, PRAYING ONLY FOR KNOWLEDGE OF HIS
WILL FOR US AND
THE POWER TO CARRY THAT OUT."
(AA & ALANON Eleventh Step)

MOM, WE WONT GET INTO DADs PAINT EVER AGAIN!

"CONTINUED TO TAKE PERSONAL
INVENTORY AND WHEN WE
WERE WRONG
PROMPTLY ADMITTED IT."
(AA & ALANON Tenth Step)

and now for a few Fun Family Fotos

"ALEXANDER FAMILY 1980"

MONICA RAY TIM DE ANN

MADELEINE REBECCA MARY LOU WENDELL THERESA CHRIS

the kids grew up . . .

LINDA
CHRIS
THERESA
DOMINIC
RAYMOND
MELONIE
BOB
REBECCA
WENDELL (In Heaven)

TIM
DEBBIE
MONICA
TED
JERRY
DEANN
DAVE Gil
MADELEINE
MARY LOU

. . . and then they got married!

ROBERT SPRING

ERIC

OWLAND ALEX KELLIE R.J.Jr. NICOLE BOBBY RICKY (In Heaven)

STEPHANIE BRIANNA YVETTE MIKIE JONATHAN MATT LINDSEY KATRINA

JENNIFER KAYLA JAIMIE

1997

. . . and then they had babies!

. . . then the girls needed a night off!

From left to right on couch:
Madeleine, Rebecca, Theresa, Monica & De Ann,
Mama Lou in front!

. . . and the boys (with Dad)
needed a ride in the ol' caddy

From left to right:
Tim, Chris, Wendell "Dear", and Ray

Finally . . . Our Remedy
For Fear & Worry!

Certificate of Enthronement

We the undersigned members of the family of

Wendell O. Alexander

Solemnly Enthroned

The Sacred Heart of Jesus as

King of Our Family

and Lovingly Consecrated its Members both Living and Dead to His

MOST SACRED HEART

on this the _15_ day of _July_, 19_62_ In Token Whereof We Sign

Father _Wendell O. Alexander_

Mother _Mary Lou Alexander_

Father Director

Children _Christopher_

Dee Ann _Raymond_

Monica _Theresa_

Priest _Rev. John F. Slattery_

CUM PERMISSU SUPERIORUM. THE FEAST OF THE SACRED HEART SHOULD BE CELEBRATED WITH GREAT SOLEMNITY AT HOME AND IN CHURCH.

Permission has been granted for the use of the form printed
on the facing page by: The National Center of the Enthronement,
Fathers of the Sacred Heart, Fairhaven, Mass. 02719

REGNUM
ADVENIAT TUUM

We the undersigned   members of the family of

_____

Solemnly Enthroned The Sacred Heart of Jesus
as
King of Our Family

and Lovingly Consecrated its Members both Living and Dead to His

MOST SACRED HEART

on this the ___ day of _____ 19 ___ In Token Whereof We Sign

Father _____   Mother _____

Children _____   Children _____

_____   _____

_____   Fr. A Wm Mitchell, ss.cc.

_____

Witness by Priest or duly Authorized Representative   National Director

THE FEAST OF THE SACRED HEART

should be celebrated with Great Solemnity in Home and in Church

Receive Holy Communion frequently   Renew your Consecration nightly,
Recite the Daily Family Rosary   on anniversaries, birthdays, deaths,
Make monthly Family Holy Hour   on First Fridays and Feastdays

NATIONAL CENTER OF THE ENTHRONEMENT
FATHERS OF THE SACRED HEARTS
FAIRHAVEN, MASS. 02719

Cum Permissu Superiorum

Treasured Memories

NEVER end . . .

once upon a long ago

each one of them was two . . .

Chris	Tim	DeAnn	Monica
Raymond	Theresa	Rebecca	Madeleine

I remember . . .

www.ingramcontent.com/pod-product-compliance
Lightning Source LLC
Chambersburg PA
CBHW081140090426
42736CB00018B/3429